BENJAMIN FRANKLIN

BENJAMIN FRANKLIN

BY L.L. OWENS

Content Consultant
Laura E. Beardsley
Independent Historian

ABDO
Publishing Company

CREDITS

Published by ABDO Publishing Company, 8000 West 78th Street, Edina, Minnesota 55439. Copyright © 2008 by Abdo Consulting Group, Inc. International copyrights reserved in all countries. No part of this book may be reproduced in any form without written permission from the publisher. The Essential Library™ is a trademark and logo of ABDO Publishing Company.

Printed in the United States.

Editor: Paula Lewis
Cover Design: Becky Daum
Interior Design: Lindaanne Donohoe

Library of Congress Cataloging-in-Publication Data
Owens, L. L.
  Benjamin Franklin / L. L. Owens.
     p. cm.—(Essential lives)
  Includes bibliographical references and index.
  ISBN 978-1-59928-840-6
  1. Franklin, Benjamin, 1706-1790—Juvenile literature. 2. Statesmen—United States—Biography—Juvenile literature. 3. Scientists—United States—Biography—Juvenile literature. 4. Inventors—United States—Biography—Juvenile literature. 5. Printers—United States—Biography—Juvenile literature. I. Title.

E302.6.F8O93 2007
973.3092—dc22
[B]

                                              2007012271

TABLE OF CONTENTS

Benjamin Franklin reading

A Self-made Man

Who was Benjamin Franklin? That may seem like an easy question to answer. For most people, Franklin's name brings to mind a successful printer, a popular writer, a famous patriot and Founding Father, and a respected scientist.

It also is easy to point to the significance of any one of Franklin's important contributions to American life. He invented the lightning rod, he started America's first fire department, and he signed the Declaration of Independence.

But even though he is one of the most famous Americans in history, it is difficult to describe Franklin's life in just a few sentences. His accomplishments are staggering. Entire libraries are devoted to housing Franklin's writings and those of others trying to capture the essence of his remarkable life.

Franklin was a practical man. He thought about his future. He loved learning and wanted to earn the freedom to pursue his many interests. And, he wanted to consciously work on being a better person. He wanted to do everything in his power to achieve personal success. To him, success meant more than just good, steady work. It meant leading a meaningful life, a life that counted.

EARLY LIFE

Benjamin Franklin was born in Boston, Massachusetts, on January 17, 1706, to Josiah and Abiah Franklin. He was the eighth of their ten children. Ben had 15 siblings and step-siblings.

Benjamin Franklin's birthplace in Boston, 1706

The six eldest Franklin children were from Josiah's first marriage. Ben was Josiah's tenth son. Josiah, his first wife, Anne, and their three children had emigrated from Ecton, England, to Boston in 1683. Boston was the busiest seaport harbor in the colonies. It also had the largest population, with 5,000 citizens. While in England, Josiah had been in the textile business, dying silks and other fine fabrics for use in items such as clothing and curtains. But demand for his skills was low in Puritan Boston, where such finery and flashiness were not considered appropriate. As a result, he had trouble finding enough work to support the family. Out of necessity, he learned a new trade. By the time Ben was born, Josiah had become a tallow chandler making soap and candles in his own shop.

The Franklin household was busy. Ben's parents liked to entertain, and the dinner conversation was always lively. Josiah was especially interested in politics and religion. He hoped his children would be too. Josiah let them listen in on the adult conversations. He thought it was important for the children to be exposed early to the ways of the world, because, as was typical of the era, children would be out of the house and on their own at a young age.

School Days

Ben was always interested in what the adults talked about, and he wanted to learn more. An avid reader, his favorite topics were science, religion, and history. He was interested in studying wartime strategies from around the world as well as the lives of important social figures.

Young Ben read all the books in the family library and borrowed others whenever he could. If he would

> "I do not remember when I could not read."[1]
>
> —*Benjamin Franklin*

have had his way, he would have read every book in Boston—and then some.

Money was tight for the Franklin family, so not much was left over to send the children to school. However, when Ben was eight, Josiah enrolled him in the Boston Latin School. He knew Ben was intelligent and had a great thirst for learning. He wanted to give the boy a chance to study. And he hoped that Ben's education would set him on the path to becoming a minister. His fondest wish was that his son would study religion at Harvard.

Ben was a gifted student. However, Josiah moved Ben to the writing and arithmetic academy. Ben excelled in writing but failed arithmetic. Josiah pulled Ben out of school after one year. Perhaps the school was too much of an added expense. But Josiah Franklin had done well for himself. Historians have suggested that Josiah simply understood that Ben was not suited for the clergy. He may have decided it was time for Ben to focus on something else.

Coming to America
Josiah Franklin and his family emigrated from England to Boston in 1683. The population of Boston at the time of Franklin's birth was approximately 8,000. Today Boston's population is 600,000—almost 75 times that of when Franklin was born.

This marked the end of Ben's short, formal education and the beginning of his long life filled with work. It was time for Ben to learn a trade of his own. Like many young boys in the early 1700s, Ben had to forgo an education and start learning a trade.

First Jobs

For about two years, Ben helped out at his father's shop. He did small jobs such as filling soap molds and cutting the wicks for the candles. He also waited on customers, made deliveries, and did other odd jobs around the store.

The work was easy enough for Ben to handle, but it was repetitive and he did not really enjoy it. He worked for a knife maker for a brief time. That did not quite suit him either. He and his father visited other tradesmen, such as silversmiths and carpenters, to determine what might be right for him. Josiah wanted Ben to work at something that interested him. Understanding how much Ben loved books and reading, Josiah felt he had come up with the perfect

An Avid Reader
Ben liked to read into the night. He read by candlelight, using the damaged and crooked candles that could not be sold in his father's shop.

Ben's favorite book was *The Pilgrim's Progress*. The story features a young man who strives to be a good person.

solution. He decided to apprentice Ben to a printer. But he did not choose just any printer. Ben's new boss was his brother, James.

Apprentice is another word for beginner or learner. When a boy was apprenticed, he would work for a tradesman such as a bricklayer, a butcher, or a printer. An apprentice would spend several years working without being paid. In exchange, he had the opportunity to learn a trade from the ground up. He would work closely with the tradesman and by the time the apprenticeship ended, he likely would be qualified to

Self-educated

Ben was forced to leave school at ten years old. His father wanted him to learn a trade. But just because Ben was no longer attending classes did not mean he stopped learning. It was quite the opposite. He studied on his own time and taught himself grammar, arithmetic, and several foreign languages. He also studied subjects such as navigation and philosophy. Ben was proud of how he had educated himself. And that self-education certainly served him well.

From a young age, Ben had an intense interest in books. They were hard to come by in the 1700s. Books were expensive and it was unusual for most people to own many. Books were a luxury item. Josiah, also a great reader, kept a small library at home. But Ben was always looking for new reading material.

Ben saved his pennies to buy a few books of his own, and he borrowed books whenever he could. He borrowed from friends, neighbors, shop customers, and apprentice booksellers— just about anyone he could think of. His desire to keep reading was so strong that he would often read late into the night. This was a habit he never outgrew.

set up his own shop.

According to the apprenticeship contract the Franklins signed, the 12-year-old Ben would work for James until he was 21. That was two years longer than the typical seven-year apprenticeship of the era.

The job was a good choice. A printer's skills included writing, editing, and setting type for pamphlets, newspapers, and books. For a boy who loved reading and working with language, the work came naturally. Ben excelled in his new position. He was a great help to James, and the business grew.

Pastime
One of Ben's favorite pastimes was swimming. An excellent swimmer, he often relied on his swimming ability as he conducted experiments with his homemade paddles and sails.

Ben not only loved to read, he also liked to discuss what he had read and voice his opinions. Soon Ben wanted to try his hand at writing. As with all his endeavors, he took this seriously. He was ready to work.

He started out writing a bit of poetry, and then he switched to essay writing. He taught himself how to write essays by studying his favorite ones from the London publication *The Spectator*. He would read the original and write his own version of the same theme. He paid careful attention to duplicating the structure of

Personal Library

Ben wanted books of his own, but for that he needed money. As a teenager, he came up with a plan to have more money for books. He noticed that meat was more expensive than foods such as bread and potatoes. So Ben became a vegetarian. The money he saved on meat then went toward the cost of building a library of his own.

the published piece. He would copy the writer's style, but substitute his own words and phrases. He would rework each piece many times. He even went so far as to convert the essays to rhyming verse and back again. Soon he was crafting essays using only his own words and ideas.

Ben was born to be a writer. And it would not be long before people were eagerly reading his work.

Young Ben was apprenticed to a printer—his brother, James.

Newspapers were a main source of information.

LEARNING A TRADE

en continued working as an apprentice to his brother James. Ben was good at his job, and James relied on him more and more. The printing business was quite successful. They handled all kinds of printing jobs, such as books, pamphlets, and advertisements. For a while, James and Ben managed the printing of the *Boston Gazette*. But after less than a year, the paper switched its business to a rival local printer.

James had enjoyed working with the *Gazette* and was upset to lose it to another printer. But this change gave him an idea. He could turn this into an opportunity to start his own newspaper. After all, he now knew what it took to put one together, and he felt he could create something unique.

The *Gazette* featured reprints of the news from abroad, many advertisements, and lots of dull reading such as long lists of contact information for government officials. But James wanted to work with fresh, local news. He also wanted to outsell the competition.

NEW ENGLAND COURANT

In August 1721, James founded the *New England Courant*, one of the first true newspapers in the colonies. His vision was to give Bostonians something to talk about. He wanted people to be so intrigued by any issue they read that they could not wait for the next.

A Virtuous Life

When Franklin was 20, he made a list of virtues to live by. He originally listed 12 virtues: temperance, silence, order, resolution, frugality, industry, sincerity, justice, moderation, cleanliness, tranquility, and chastity.

Upon reading the list, one of Ben's friends said that Ben was often guilty of being overbearing and insolent. That is when Ben added the thirteenth virtue: humility.

Setting type by hand in a print shop

He hoped the *Courant* would become the source for exciting local news, from individual triumphs and tragedies to all the latest town gossip and political talk.

Ben worked by his brother's side in this new project. James gave him quite a bit of responsibility too. Besides delivering the finished paper, Ben also set the type and printed the pages. Typesetting and printing were time-consuming tasks and required keen attention to detail. There were no typewriters, computers, or digital printers. Ben did all of it by hand. He worked letter by letter, line by line, story by story, and page by page for each weekly issue.

For each story, Ben lined up the individual metal letters in a tray. These looked similar to rubber stamps you might find today. Words had to be composed working from right to left so the printed copy would read from left to right. Franklin had to read backward in order to check his work. Ink was applied to the "set type," and the page was transferred, or printed, onto paper. Ben printed as many copies of one page as he would need for all the customers in Boston. Then he repeated the process for each additional page of the newspaper.

Extra Income
For fun, Ben sometimes wrote historical ballads and sold printed versions out of his brother's print shop.

The lively, entertaining *Courant* was well received. Some Bostonians were initially shocked by its bold content. Nonetheless, they were eager to read it. The most popular features were the political satires James and his friends wrote. The paper always included pointed articles, letters from the readers, and editorials that made fun of political leaders and their questionable activities.

To protect their identities (which did not necessarily work), James and the other writers used false names, or pseudonyms. They usually disguised the names of those they wrote about too. One of the names that James used was Homespun Jack, a man who hated the local fashions, particularly the tiny waists that the ladies favored.

He also used the name Tom Tram, who supposedly wrote from his desk on the moon about the evil local post-master. Ichabod Henroost ranted about the pressures of living with a nagging wife. And Timothy Turnstone criticized the integrity of Justice Nicholas Clodplate.

THE SILENCE DOGOOD LETTERS

During this exciting period, Ben

Silence Dogood

From April through October 1722, Ben wrote many letters to the *New England Courant*. Instead of signing his own name, he used the name Silence Dogood. That false name is what is known as a pseudonym.

Ben was not the first to disguise his identity. In the 1700s, it was common for writers to use a different name when they wrote something controversial. Others used several pseudonyms at once. Sometimes a newspaper had only one or two people writing the articles, but wanted it to appear as though there were many writers. Or a writer felt his various points of view might be more believable coming from different character types.

Silence Dogood may have been Ben's first pseudonym, but it was far from his last. He wrote under many names throughout his life. For each one, Ben assumed a different character for the writing. His readers often knew the character's supposed background. There was no mistaking the character's opinions. This gave Ben more freedom to express his views, whether they were political or humorous jabs at people or ideas he found silly.

Ben's Mrs. Dogood was a 40-year-old widow with strong opinions. She wrote 14 letters to the *New England Courant*.

---

thought that he, too, might like to
become a writer. He was growing
bored with his normal duties at the
paper and wanted to try more creative
work. He practiced writing on his
own, hoping to one day impress James
with his talent. He knew, though, that
James would not be interested in
looking at his writings at first. Ben
came up with a plan to test the waters.

Letters from Mrs. Dogood

Silence Dogood was Ben's first pseudonym, and James had no idea the letters were written by his younger brother. Mrs. Dogood introduced herself in a letter published April 2, 1722.

He would disguise his writing and submit letters to the
paper using a different name. James would never know
it was him. Thus, the middle-aged widow, Silence
Dogood, became 16-year-old Ben's first pseudonym.

Silence Dogood wrote a letter to the paper giving
information about her background and reasons for
writing. She promised to provide *New England Courant*
readers with entertaining letters focusing on whatever
she found interesting in Boston. The letter was slipped
under the door of the print shop.

James was thrilled to get letters from readers. It
meant that people were reading the *Courant*. It also
meant just a little less work for his busy staff. He and
the readers could not wait for Mrs. Dogood's next
letter.

In all, Ben produced 14 letters as Silence Dogood. He wrote about everything from Harvard students to politics to the courtship rituals of Boston's youth. The pieces were witty, current, and a hit with readers.

Ben was proud of his success and loved listening to people trying to guess the writer's true identity. James and his other employees often supposed that Mrs. Dogood was a person of great character and considerable education.

James never suspected that Ben was his favorite contributor. He truly had no idea that he was publishing his brother's writings. Ben continued to hide the truth because of his strong instinct that James would never take him seriously as a writer. Nor would he support the notion of Ben receiving any recognition.

By all accounts, Ben's instinct was right. Ben's anonymous success and growing impatience with taking orders from James caused him to resent the terms of his apprenticeship. He could not imagine continuing for several more years.

This was the beginning of a serious rift between the Franklin brothers. Reportedly, James was jealous of Ben's talents. And Ben resented James. He thought

Learning the Trade

Ben learned many skills of the printing trade working as an apprentice to his brother James. His father had made a good choice.

James took his work at the print shop for granted. He was angered that James did not want to see him succeed. James started treating Ben more harshly and became more hostile. James accused Ben of doing a poor job and made him work longer hours. The brothers regularly argued, and sometimes the disagreements became physical.

Soon James had to deal with more than just sibling rivalry and bad feelings. His business was about to be threatened, and he would need to turn to Ben for help. Ben was ready for the challenge.

Ben Takes Charge

All the thinly disguised attacks on recognizable authority figures being printed in the *Courant* were bound to cause trouble for the paper. The governor of Massachusetts did not like being criticized in the *Courant*, and he took it out on its publisher. James was sent to jail for one month. He asked Ben to keep the newspaper running.

Ben put together an entire issue all by himself. He was just 17 years old, but he did it all, from the editing to the printing. And Ben did it well.

James was released from jail, but quickly found himself back in trouble. He was barred from working

A Farewell Letter
James eventually started to suspect that Ben might be behind the Silence Dogood letters. And Ben knew it. Not wanting to be caught, Silence Dogood quickly wrote a good-bye letter to her public.

on the paper, so he asked Ben for help again. James wanted to run the paper in secret and have Ben act as if he was running it. This was the last straw for Ben. He might have liked to run the newspaper for real, but he had no interest in only playing the part, especially since James would still expect him to take orders. He was tired of being mistreated and undervalued by his brother. And he was done being an apprentice. He knew he could find a better situation.

Unfortunately, Ben also knew he could not find what he was looking for in Boston. To follow his dreams, he would need to leave his hometown.

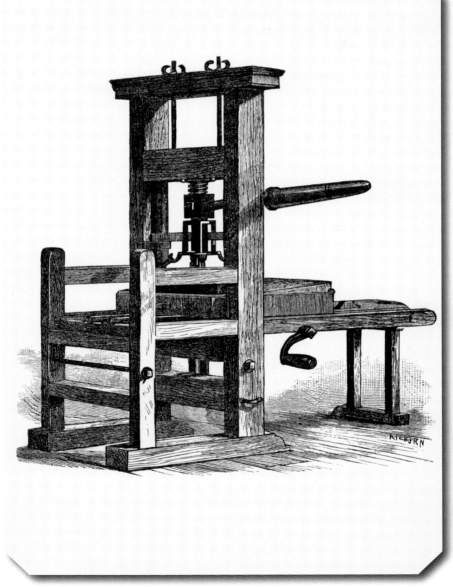

An early printing press

Ben Franklin entering Philadelphia as a young man

ON HIS OWN

en knew it was time to leave his apprenticeship. He was unhappy working for James and wanted to seek his own fortune. He was confident in the skills he had learned at the print shop and thought they would serve him well.

However, everyone in Boston knew Ben. Leaving an apprenticeship would be looked down upon. Other businessmen would not want to hire someone who had broken a contract. Ben was also afraid that James would make life difficult for him. In his mind, the only real option was to run away.

The Runaway

Ben waited for the right time to leave. He chose New York as his destination because he knew of a printer there. He sold some of his books to raise money for the trip. Ben's good friend, John Collins, helped him arrange for passage on a boat leaving Boston Harbor on September 25, 1723.

Ben sneaked away that day and quietly boarded the boat. He was ready to leave behind his home, his family, and the life he had known. Ben was only 17 years old.

Shortly after arriving in New York, he made contact with a printer named William Bradford. Although Bradford had no work for the young man, he suggested that Ben try his luck in Philadelphia.

Help Wanted

Just days after Ben ran away and left his apprenticeship behind, Ben's brother placed the following ad in the September 30, 1723, *New England Courant*:

"James Franklin, printer in Queen Street, wants a likely lad for an apprentice."[1]

By October 8, just a couple of weeks after leaving Boston, Ben had made his way to Philadelphia—the city that would be most closely associated with his legacy.

Ben arrived with just three cents to his name. With that, he bought three large bread rolls and set about finding the printing shop Bradford had mentioned.

Unfortunately, no job was available, but he did not give up. He visited the only other print shop in town and was hired on the spot by owner Samuel Keimer.

Good fortune would follow Ben throughout his life. People were drawn to his natural

An Eventful Trip

When Ben was only 17 years old, he struck out on his own in September 1723. He tried his luck in New York before heading to Philadelphia. The cities were approximately 100 miles (160 km) apart, but Ben's journey turned into an experience he would never forget.

Ben boarded a small, dilapidated sailboat in New York Harbor, thinking the voyage to Philadelphia would be quick and uneventful. When a violent storm came up, the old boat was thrown off course. As the boat seesawed in the rough waters, one of the passengers lost his balance and fell overboard. Ben reached into the water and pulled the man—by his hair—back to safety. The storm continued, making it impossible for the little boat to safely land. So Ben and the others spent a long, wet night waiting for an opportunity to take the boat ashore. Everyone huddled together in the cold.

The boat finally reached New Jersey the next morning. Ben learned that he could catch another boat to Philadelphia in Burlington—50 miles (80 km) away. With little rest, no horse, and little money, he started walking. On October 8, an exhausted Ben finally made it to Philadelphia.

intelligence and charm, and they often went out of their way to help him. In the biography *Benjamin Franklin: An American Life*, author Walter Isaacson describes Ben's appeal:

> At 17, Franklin was physically striking: muscular, barrel-chested, open-faced, and almost six feet tall. He had the happy talent of being at ease in almost any company, from scrappy tradesman to wealthy merchants, scholars to rogues. His most notable trait was a personal magnetism; he attracted people who wanted to help him. Never shy, and always eager to win friends and patrons, he gregariously exploited this charm.[2]

Ben took up residence in a boardinghouse run by John Read. It was there that he first met his future wife, Read's daughter, Deborah. He enjoyed her company and looked forward to spending time with her when he had a bit of time off work.

But Ben worked hard. He put in long hours for Keimer. He had learned the printing trade inside and out during his apprenticeship, and his expertise was recognized. Keimer rewarded Ben by giving him more

Brotherly Love
The name Philadelphia means "brotherly love" in Greek. William Penn founded the city in 1682. A Quaker, Penn wanted the city to embody the principles of freedom and religious tolerance.

Governor Keith suggests Ben start a printing shop in England.

responsibility at the shop. Though still very young, Ben became well known as Philadelphia's most skilled printer. His apprenticeship had paid off.

OPPORTUNITY KNOCKS

Pennsylvania's governor, Sir William Keith, was a friend of Ben's brother-in-law. Keith had heard that Ben's family worried about him and wanted him to come home to Boston. After reading one of Ben's letters about his determination to succeed, the governor was impressed. He admired young Ben's maturity and ambition. So he set up a meeting with Ben to discuss a business proposal.

Keith wanted Ben to start his own printing shop. He promised to give Ben an exclusive contract for printing the state's official documents.

This opportunity sounded good to Ben. He wondered, though, how he could raise the money he would need to go into business. He asked his father for assistance, but Josiah refused.

Keith was so keen to work with Ben that he offered to finance the business himself. His condition was that Ben visit London to make new business connections. While there, Ben could buy all the equipment he needed. Keith assured Ben that he would send letters of introduction to all the people he would need to meet.

Ben agreed to Keith's terms and prepared to set sail for England. Before leaving, he became engaged to Deborah Read. The pair wanted to wed right away, but Deborah's mother

A New Home

Philadelphia had a population of about 10,000 when Ben moved there in 1723. At that time, the city was just 50 years old and growing quickly in size and in importance.

Ben would spend much of his adult life calling Philadelphia home. It was ethnically and religiously diverse compared to some other colonial cities, including the Puritanical Boston. The liberal atmosphere suited Ben.

asked them to wait until Ben returned from London. Ben thought he would be away for just a short time, so that seemed like a reasonable plan. The couple vowed to marry as soon as Ben came back to Philadelphia.

When Ben arrived in London, he found that Keith had not upheld his end of their bargain. He had no access to the funds or to the people that Keith had promised. Luckily, Ben found work with a London printer as a typesetter and was able to support himself.

LIFE IN LONDON

When Ben was not working, he attended the theater and the opera. He also became well acquainted with London's libraries, coffee houses, and taverns. He spent time with a friend who had also made the trip from Philadelphia. To young men of 18 and 19, the vibrant, bustling city held much appeal.

While Ben did enjoy himself in London, he remained true to his strong work ethic. He worked hard at the printing shop. He also took the time to write and publish his own pamphlet in response to a book his

London

In late 1724, 18-year-old Ben left Philadelphia to try to make business contacts in London. With a population of about 700,000, London was Europe's largest city.

Ben's ship arrived on Christmas Eve. His original plan did not work out, and he stayed in London for nearly two years before returning home.

shop had printed. The book was *The Religion of Nature Delineated* by William Wollaston. The author presented the controversial idea that the study of science and nature was the best way to discover religious truths.

Ben wrote the pamphlet *A Dissertation on Liberty and Necessity, Pleasure and Pain*. His goal was to call out which parts of Wollaston's theory held up and which parts did not. It was a heavy undertaking for Ben, and he had a difficult time following the original arguments from beginning to end. But for someone so young and inexperienced at philosophizing, it was a great effort.

Following is a sample from Ben's dissertation. He responded to Wollaston's assertion that if God is all-powerful, then nothing in the universe can happen without his consent—and therefore every happening must be good because evil cannot exist:

> *It will be said, perhaps, that God permits evil actions to be done, for wise ends and purposes. But this objection destroys itself; for whatever and infinitely good God hath wise ends in suffering to be, must be good, is thereby made good, and cannot be otherwise.*[3]

Ben distributed 100 copies of the pamphlet. Then he reread his work and decided his arguments were shallow and unconvincing. So he set about getting back and burning all the copies of the dissertation he could possibly find.

A short time later, Ben took a new position with a different London printer. But he was not certain that he wanted to stay in that job, or even in London. His career was not on the kind of stable footing he had hoped for. To make ends meet, he even considered working as a swimming instructor. However, an offer from Thomas Denham, his friend from the voyage over, to work as a store clerk in Philadelphia was just the break he needed. On July 2, 1726, after three years on his own, 20-year-old Ben boarded a ship for home.

Men congregating in London taverns

Philadelphia, 1726

BACK IN PHILADELPHIA

Franklin arrived in Philadelphia on October 11, 1726, after two and a half months at sea. Deborah Read had surprising news for him. She had married someone else while he was working in London.

Deborah had tired of waiting for Ben. She had heard from him only once and had come to believe he would never return from London. She married a potter named John Rogers, hoping to start a life with him. Soon, though, she discovered that Rogers had more than one wife. He was a polygamist. Wanting no part of a marriage in which she would have to share her husband, Deborah left Rogers immediately and began using her maiden name.

Franklin was shocked to hear her story. He was saddened that she had felt he had forgotten about her, but in truth, he had been focused on other things. While he was in London, life in Philadelphia seemed part of a different world. On the same continent again at last, Ben and Deborah found they still loved each other. The couple decided to resume their courtship. They would go on to marry but not right away.

Now that Franklin was back in the colonies, he had to support himself. He went to work for shop owner Thomas Denham, who sold English goods to colonists who missed the products of their homeland.

The Face on the $100 Bill

Franklin helped design and print paper currency as part of his job. But he could not have imagined that one day his likeness would be on the $100 bill. The "Benjamin" is the largest denomination of U.S. currency used today.

Business was profitable, and Franklin learned a lot in his salesman position. He also formed a close relationship with Denham. The older gentleman treated him like a son. When Denham died several months later, Franklin was devastated. He had lost a father figure. He had also lost a job, as Denham's shop was forced to close upon his death.

Franklin accepted a position working for printer Samuel Keimer, his former boss. Keimer trusted him, placing him in charge of running the shop and training new employees. During his time at Keimer's shop, Franklin helped with a major project. Keimer was awarded the contract to print the colonies' first paper currency. Franklin designed and built a new copperplate press for the job. He helped design the bills, too.

The Junto Club

As usual, Franklin continued to pursue other interests outside of work. He loved to engage in stimulating discussions about world affairs. In 1727, he established the Junto club. Franklin's goal was to create a social group for local tradesmen and artisans who were committed to improving society. To gain acceptance into the club, prospective members had to

Ben Franklin's image appears on today's $100 bills.

correctly answer four questions. Franklin had devised these questions as a test of a person's character and belief system.

The questions (and correct answers) were:

1. *Have you any disrespect to any present member? (No.)*

2. *Do you sincerely love mankind in general of what profession or religion soever? (Yes.)*

3. *Do you think any person should ever be punished because of their opinions or religion? (No.)*

4. *Do you love truth for its own sake? (Yes.)*[1]

The Junto members met every Friday night to socialize and talk about business, politics, education, philosophy, and religion—the pressing social matters of the day. The club was also a great way for members to meet others who could help further their careers. It became a staple for the working men of Philadelphia. The meetings were held at a local pub until the group raised enough money to rent a room in a house.

Franklin was always striving for self-improvement, and he wanted the Junto members to feel that they could do the same in the supportive atmosphere of the club. Each

Junto Members

Franklin was keen on learning other people's opinions. The first Junto members were a diverse group of businessmen. These members included a: surveyor, book collector, shoemaker, a glazier (a person who works with glass), a cabinet maker, a scribe who created handwritten copies of text, and even an astrologer.

The Junto club was nicknamed the "Leather Apron Club" because most members wore leather aprons on the job, such as a blacksmith.

member was required to share a personal essay on any topic once every three months.

Junto—or the "Leather Apron Club," as it was known informally—was active in Philadelphia for the next 40 years. It helped foster a sense of community among local businessmen, and it greatly enhanced Franklin's visibility as a public figure.

The Young Printer

By 1728, Franklin was ready to start his own printing business. He launched it with the financial help of a partner but was able to take over as sole proprietor within a year. His plans were coming together.

Philadelphia already had two established printers, opening a new print shop was risky. But Franklin forged ahead and made a great success of his business.

> **What Did Franklin Look Like as a Young Man?**
> There are no early likenesses of Benjamin Franklin, but some have tried to imagine what Franklin looked like as a young man. Biographer Carl Van Doren based his educated guess about Franklin's appearance on later portraits and random notes that refer to his looks. He said this is how he would have expected Franklin to look around the time he returned to Philadelphia from London:
> *Strongly built, rounded like a swimmer or a wrestler, not angular like a runner, he was five feet nine or ten inches tall, with a large head and square, deft hands. His hair was blond or light brown, his eyes grey, full, and steady, his mouth wide and humorous with a pointed upper lip. His clothing was as clean as it was plain. Though he and others say he was hesitant in speech, he was prompt in action.[2]*

Clients felt he did the best work in town. They also saw him as the hardest-working printer. That is not to say that the others did not work hard—it is just that Ben had earned his business and his reputation by consciously doing his best at all times. He was driven to succeed.

Franklin worked long, exhausting

hours. He attributed his
accomplishments in large part to the
fact that others saw him as a hard
worker. Clients and other merchants
regularly saw Franklin start his day
early and end it very late. His
employees witnessed how hard he
would work to do the job right. He always "went the
extra mile" to achieve efficiency and quality. This set
him apart enough to get noticed. One local observer
said,

"Early to bed and early to
rise makes a man healthy,
wealthy, and wise."[4]
— *Benjamin Franklin*

> *For the industry of that Franklin, is superior to anything I
> ever saw of the kind. I see him still at work when I go home
> from club, and he is at work again before his neighbours are
> out of bed.*[3]

With his printing shop firmly established, Franklin
was eager for a fresh challenge. His new goal was to get
into the newspaper business. But that would take some
doing, as there were already two weekly newspapers in
town. Andrew Bradford owned the *American Weekly
Mercury*, and Franklin's former boss Samuel Keimer had
started the *Pennsylvania Gazette* after learning of Franklin's
plan to enter the newspaper business. It was unlikely
that the market could support three papers at the same

time. So Franklin decided to align with one of the existing publications in a bid to drive the other out of business. It was an easy choice to make considering the bitter falling out between Franklin and Keimer a couple of years earlier.

Franklin started writing for Bradford's *Mercury* and launched his attack on Keimer's *Gazette*. Keimer had recently published entries from an encyclopedia. Franklin chose an entry on "abortion" to use for his attack on Keimer.

Using the pseudonyms Martha Careful and Celia Shortface, he published mock angry letters in the rival

A Success

The first colonial newspaper originated in 1704, two years before Franklin was born. When Franklin took over the *Pennsylvania Gazette* from Keimer, only 90 people were subscribers. Making a success of a newspaper was difficult. Half of the colonial newspapers failed within two years.

Mercury. Martha and Celia raised strong objections to seeing such shocking, distasteful content in the *Gazette*.

Franklin got what he had wanted, he stirred up controversy about Keimer's paper. This incident marked the first documented abortion debate in the colonies. It also marked the beginning of the end of Keimer's *Gazette*. His readership steadily dropped, and it became difficult to continue funding it. He gave up and sold the paper to Franklin in 1729. As owner, publisher, and printer, Franklin oversaw every detail. For years, he even did much of the writing.

FAMILY LIFE

As a thriving printer and newly minted publisher of a popular newspaper, Franklin was ready to settle down. He and Deborah had been seeing each other off and on since his return from London. They now decided to enter into a common-law marriage.

A Better Name
Franklin took over as owner and publisher of his own newspaper in 1729. He bought it from rival Samuel Keimer. Franklin shortened its original name of *Universal Instructor in All Arts and Sciences, and Pennsylvania Gazette* to simply the *Pennsylvania Gazette*.

Deborah moved into Franklin's home on September 1, 1730, along with Franklin's young son, William. The child was born sometime between 1728 and 1730. Historians differ on William's year of birth and whether Deborah was the boy's birth mother. But there is no doubt that Deborah raised him as her own.

Deborah was a devoted wife and mother. She gave birth to Francis and Sarah, whom they affectionately called "Franky" and "Sally." Deborah stayed busy raising the children, supporting Franklin's many endeavors, and running a general store out of the print shop. She sold a variety of items such as paper and ink, coffee, tea, cheese, and chocolate. She even sold a specialty soap made by Franklin's family in Boston.

Franklin relied on his wife. He openly appreciated her many contributions to their home life and his career. Like her husband, Deborah was a hard worker, and her dedication helped provide Franklin with the freedom he needed to secure his place in American history.

Benjamin Franklin at his printing press in Philadelphia

A colonist reading in a private library, circa 1700

READING AND WRITING

ow in his mid-twenties, Benjamin Franklin was a respected businessman, noted writer, and solid family man. But he was just getting started. The 1730s would lay the groundwork for his roles as a great patriot and statesman.

The Library Company of Philadelphia

A community project close to Franklin's heart took shape in 1731. Books were still scarce and expensive in Philadelphia. At the time, only a few citizens had the opportunity to read books outside of a school setting. While Franklin thought everyone might like to read for pleasure, it was unusual for the average person to have access to books. There were no bookstores or public libraries in Philadelphia.

Members of the Junto club routinely traded books with each other. Franklin's general store stocked a few specialty titles as well. But Franklin had something else in mind. He proposed that the Junto club start a subscription library called the Library Company of Philadelphia.

The group began with 50 members and anyone could join for a small fee. Membership dues paid for the library's first set of 45 well-known books on subjects including history, politics, and science. And, unlike the books in colleges, these books were written in English, not Latin. The books were ordered from London and within months, members were able to borrow the books. Franklin wrote the library's motto:

To pour forth benefits for the common good is divine.[1]

Building a Community
During his years in Philadelphia, Franklin:

- Was instrumental in getting the streets paved.
- Organized the first volunteer fire brigade.
- Helped establish an orphanage.
- Proposed a university and a hospital.
- Organized a state militia.
- Founded the Junto club, the public library, and a fire insurance company.

Franklin gave so much of his time and talent to the city. The names Benjamin Franklin and Philadelphia are forever linked.

This motto was also one of his most closely held personal beliefs. He hoped to see the library thrive and attract people to the benefits and pleasures of reading. Paying members could check out books; anyone was welcome to read from the collection while visiting the library site.

The idea was a success. Both the subscriber list and book collection grew. The first books were mainly on religion and education. Later additions included poetry, science, and history books. Franklin was proud, and rightfully so. He had founded the first public library in the colonies and helped create a new community of readers. As he wrote years later in his autobiography:

Reading became fashionable. Our people having no public amusements to divert their attention from study became better acquainted with books, and in a few years were observed by strangers to be better instructed and more intelligent than people of the same rank generally are in other countries. [2]

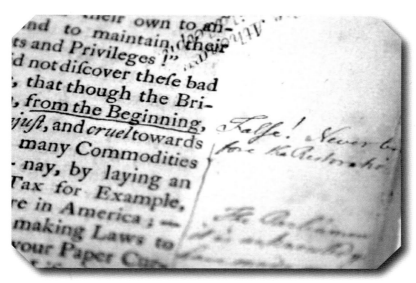

Books once owned by Benjamin Franklin often include his personal notes.

POOR RICHARD'S ALMANACK

Just one year after the successful launch of the public library, Franklin started writing what would become his most famous publishing project, *Poor Richard's Almanack*.

An almanac is an annual publication of practical information about the weather, astronomy, and important dates for the year. In Franklin's day, farmers, avid gardeners, sailors, and fishermen needed that information to plan their work. Traditionally, an almanac also offers wise and witty sayings. This made it a terrific outlet for Franklin's writing. He publicized

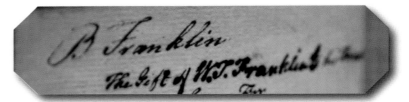

*Shown is Benjamin Franklin's signature, which is in a book
from a collection of titles once owned by Franklin.*

the almanac with a large ad in his *Pennsylvania Gazette*:

> *Poor Richard: An Almanack containing the lunations,
> eclipses, planets motions and aspects, weather, sun and
> moon's rising and setting, highwater, etc. besides many
> pleasant and witty verses, jests and sayings.*[3]

Franklin adopted the pseudonym Richard Saunders
from which the almanac took its name. "Poor Richard"
wrote a humorous introduction for each edition of the
book. He shared bits and pieces about his life as a
poverty-stricken man who loved to learn and whose wife
was a nag. He even complained about his greedy
printer, a man named Ben Franklin.

Franklin released the first edition in late 1732. It was
wildly popular and sold so well that he released three
printings of it between December 1732 and January
1733. For many colonists, the almanac was the only
book they bought each year. Most appreciated the truly
useful information Franklin included. And of course,

everyone enjoyed the delightful sayings sprinkled throughout each issue. The almanac was a wonderful showcase of his intelligence and wit. Sayings from the almanacs include:

- *Fish and visitors stink after three days.*

- *Three may keep a secret, if two of them are dead.*

- *If you would not be forgotten*
  As soon as you are dead and rotten,
  Either write things worthy reading,
  Or do things worth the writing.

- *Well done is better than well said.*

- *Glass, China, and Reputation, are easily crack'd, and never well mended.*

- *A little neglect may breed great mischief … for want of a nail the shoe was lost; for want of a shoe the horse was lost; and for want of a horse the rider was lost.*

- *Genius without education is like silver in the mine.*

- *When the well's dry, we know the worth of water.*

- *Tim was so learned, that he could name a horse in nine Languages. So ignorant, that he bought a cow to ride on.*

Big Seller

Written and published by Benjamin Franklin, *Poor Richard's Almanack* was hugely popular in the colonies. The annual publication sold about 10,000 copies a year from late 1732 to 1757.

◆ The sleeping Fox catches no poultry.

◆ Fear not death; for the sooner we die, the longer shall we be immortal.

◆ An ounce of prevention is worth a pound of cure.

◆ A country man between two lawyers, is like a fish between two cats.

◆ He that lieth down with Dogs, shall rise up with Fleas.

◆ The worst wheel of a cart makes the most noise.

◆ Love your Neighbour; yet don't pull down your Hedge.[4]

Poor Richard's Almanack

Benjamin Franklin was known for his sharp sense of humor. In the preface to the 1733 edition of *Poor Richard's Almanack*, Franklin shared his reasons for writing the books. He wrote from the fictional character Richard Saunders's point of view:

Courteous Reader,

I might in this place attempt to gain thy Favour, by declaring that I write Almanacks with no other View than that of the publick Good; ... The plain Truth of the Matter is, I am excessive poor, and my Wife, Good Woman, is, I tell her, excessive proud; she cannot bear, she says, to sit spinning in her Shift of Tow, while I do nothing but gaze at the stars; and has threatened more than once to burn all my Books and Rattling-Traps (as she calls my Instruments) if I do not make some profitable Use of them for the good of my Family The Printer has offer'd me some considerable share of the Profits, and I have thus begun to comply with my Dame's desire.[5]

Franklin was always quick to note that he did not create all the sayings that people loved so much. Many, he said, were the

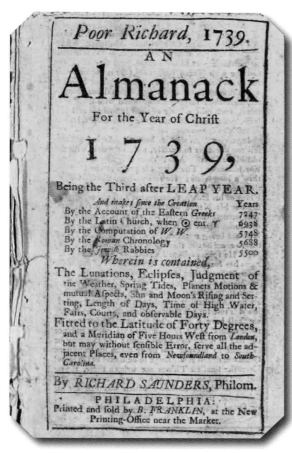

Poor Richard, 1739.

AN

Almanack

For the Year of Chrift

1 7 3 9,

Being the Third after LEAP YEAR.

And makes fince the Creation Years
By the Account of the Eaftern *Greeks* 7247
By the Latin Church, when ☉ ent. ♈ 6938
By the Computation of *W. W.* 5748
By the *Roman* Chronology 5688
By the *Jewifh* Rabbies 5500

Wherein is contained,

The Lunations, Eclipfes, Judgment of the Weather, Spring Tides, Planets Motions & mutual Afpects, Sun and Moon's Rifing and Setting, Length of Days, Time of High Water, Fairs, Courts, and obfervable Days.

Fitted to the Latitude of Forty Degrees, and a Meridian of Five Hours Weft from *London,* but may without fenfible Error, ferve all the adjacent Places, even from *Newfoundland* to *South Carolina.*

By RICHARD SAUNDERS, Philom.

PHILADELPHIA:

Printed and fold by *B. FRANKLIN,* at the New Printing-Office near the Market.

The cover page of "Poor Richard: An Almanack,"
1739 by "Richard Saunders"

"wisdom of many ages and nations"[6] and that he merely communicated them with a humorous spin. *Poor Richard's Almanack* was published each year from 1732 to 1757.

In his autobiography, Franklin wrote about the almanac that would make him both wealthy and famous:

In 1732 I first published my Almanack, under the name of Richard Saunders; it was continu'd by me about 25 Years, commonly call'd Poor Richard's Almanack. I endeavor'd to make it both entertaining and useful, and it accordingly came to be in such Demand that I reap'd considerable Profit from it, vending annually near ten Thousand. ... I consider'd it as a proper Vehicle for conveying Instruction among the common People, who bought scarcely any other Books. I therefore filled all the little Spaces that occur'd between the Remarkable Days in the Calendar, with Proverbial Sentences, chiefly such as inculcated Industry and Frugality, as the Means of procuring Wealth and thereby securing Virtue, it being more difficult for a Man in Want to act always honestly, as (to use here one of those Proverbs) it is hard for an empty Sack to stand upright.[7]

Benjamin Franklin in his twenties

An 1847 postage stamp of Benjamin Franklin

Community Service

he Franklins' four-year-old son, Franky, was a bright, curious boy with whom Franklin felt a special connection. But in 1736, life took a depressing turn for Benjamin and Deborah Franklin. They suffered the devastating loss of their young son to smallpox.

Franklin never got over his grief and throughout the rest of his life carried guilt over Franky's death. Smallpox is a contagious and usually deadly disease. There are no treatments or cures. For years, Franklin had been a vocal supporter of the smallpox vaccination. He had written about the clear benefits of the vaccine. He had campaigned for its widespread use. Yet, somehow, he failed to inoculate his own son. Ironically, Franklin is credited with the quote, "An ounce of prevention is worth a pound of cure."[1] The touching tribute on Franky's gravestone read, "The delight of all who knew him."[2]

ENTERING POLITICS

That same year, Franklin was elected clerk of the Pennsylvania Assembly. It was his first political role and was followed by his appointment as Philadelphia's postmaster in 1737. This was the beginning of a long history with the postal service.

The Franklin Family
Benjamin and Deborah Franklin had a small family by the standards of the mid-eighteenth century. While Franklin had 15 siblings and half-siblings, and Deborah had six, they raised just three children. William was the eldest son, born around 1730. Francis was born in 1732 and died of smallpox at age four. The Franklins' only daughter, Sarah, was born in 1743.

He gained even more visibility as a public servant, and his printing business benefited from his ability to use the postal system to his advantage.

The previous postmaster, fellow printer and *American Weekly Mercury* publisher Andrew Bradford, had prevented Franklin from distributing the *Pennsylvania Gazette* through the mail. Bradford unfairly ruled on the issue with the intention of limiting Franklin's sales. Franklin had reacted by bribing individual postal riders to deliver the *Gazette.* But now that Franklin was postmaster, he could make some real changes. He wrote about his eager acceptance of the position:

> I accepted it readily, and found it of great advan-tage, for though the salary was small, it

Postmaster

The United States Postal Service celebrated the 300th anniversary of Benjamin Franklin's birth by issuing four commemorative 39-cent stamps in his honor. The announcement was made on January 17, 2006, and the stamps went on sale in Philadelphia later that spring.

Images on the stamps depict Franklin in his roles as statesman, scientist, printer, and—perhaps the most meaningful role in the eyes of the postal service—postmaster.

The postmaster stamp features an eighteenth-century painting of Franklin. It is highlighted with images of a 1775 letter to Philadelphia, a colonial postmark, and a graphic used by the *Boston Post-Boy* newspaper in the mid-1700s. Educational text behind the plate of the postmaster stamp reads:

> Benjamin Franklin was vital to the organization of the American postal system, serving as postmaster of Philadelphia and a Deputy Postmaster for the American colonies before being appointed Postmaster General by the Continental Congress in 1775. He marked postage free letters with his unique personal signature: "B. Free Franklin"[3]

*facilitated the correspondence that improved my newspaper,
increased the number demanded, as well as the advertisements to be inserted, so that it came to afford me a very
considerable income.* [4]

Franklin's new policies made it possible for Bradford
to also promote his paper through the postal system.
However, the *Mercury* failed to keep pace with the *Gazette*.
Competition between the Philadelphia printers
remained heated. But Franklin
definitely came out as the winner. And,
Franklin's many successes changed the
scope of the profession and shed light
on its great potential for profitability.

Daughter Sally

In 1743, the Franklin family grew
with the birth of daughter Sarah, who
they affectionately called Sally. It had
been several years since Franky's tragic
death, and the Franklins welcomed a new life into the
household. By this time, big brother William was about
13. Baby Sally was a smart, charming girl, and Franklin
took great pleasure in watching her grow. Still hurting
from Franky's death, Franklin made sure to inoculate
his precious daughter against smallpox when she was a

Mail Service
Franklin was proud to be
Deputy Postmaster Gen-
eral of North America.
He took his responsibil-
ity for the colonial mail
services seriously and
worked to make im-
provements. One of his
accomplishments was
the establishment of a
24-hour mail service
between Philadelphia,
Boston, and New York.

toddler. He proudly wrote about six-year-old Sally to his mother:

> Sally grows a fine Girl, and is extremely industrious with her Needle, and delights in her book. She is of most affectionate Temper, and perfectly Dutiful and obliging, to her Parents and to all. Perhaps I flatter myself to much, but I have Hopes that she will prove an ingenious, sensible, notable, and Worthy woman ...[5]

AMERICAN PHILOSOPHICAL SOCIETY

Franklin continued serving his community throughout the 1740s. Having had great success with forming the business-oriented Junto club, Franklin looked toward starting a new kind of organization. His work as Philadelphia's postmaster increased his contact with the other colonies. And, he had recently started exploring the idea of uniting the separate American colonies while still remaining a part of the British Empire. What better way to study the issue (among others), he thought, than through a club made up of members from different colonies?

In the spring of 1743, Franklin founded the American Philosophical Society. Colonial leaders

A guide to smallpox treatment in New England ca. 1700

would share ideas on all manner of important issues. Franklin hoped to create an environment for scientists, philosophers, mathematicians, and other great thinkers to study common community problems. His hope was that the society would create solutions to be shared among the colonies. He felt this would encourage the separate colonies to think and work together as a unit.

At this point, Franklin could not have predicted that the colonies would one day present a united front to fight for independence from Britain.

At first, the group corresponded through the post by trading letters, essays, and research studies. By the spring of 1744, they were meeting regularly in Philadelphia.

PENNSYLVANIA MILITIA

As part of his quest to help Pennsylvania prepare to defend itself in the event of an outside invasion, Franklin suggested the formation of a volunteer army. The Pennsylvania Militia started in 1747. The colonies had faced occasional threats from Spain and France. Colonists had been unhappy with the government's response to these threats. The Pennsylvania Assembly had refused to fund a militia. People wanted to know that at least a citizens' group existed that was organized and ready to defend the land.

Franklin promoted the concept of a militia and wrote a pamphlet titled *Plain Truth*. In it, he stressed that the colonists could protect themselves. He said it was up to the tradesmen and other ordinary men to act where their government would not. He recalled a proverb that noted the English might not be counted upon to help them:

> [They] are sensible of inconveniences when they are present, but do not take sufficient care to prevent them: their natural courage makes them too little apprehensive of danger, so that they are often surprised by it, unprovided of the proper means of security. [6]

Franklin also wrote:

> At present we are like separate filaments of flax before the thread is formed, without strength because without connection. But Union would make us strong. [7]

Franklin's words struck a chord with the citizenry, who realized that attack was possible. They wanted the means to protect themselves. More than 10,000 men volunteered to serve in the militia, forming approximately 100 companies across the colony.

Franklin refused a position of leadership, preferring to serve as a regular soldier in the Philadelphia unit. He made significant contributions to the cause. He helped raise money for weaponry and other supplies, and he wrote detailed rules for the militia's training practices

and regular operations. He also wrote
the charter for the organization, saying
they had formed because they were

Retirement

Franklin retired from business in 1748. His successful printing business had been profitable, and he had shrewdly invested his money in Philadelphia property and several colonial printing shops.

> *thus unprotected by the government
> under which we live, we do hereby, for
> our mutual defense and security, and for
> the security of our wives, children, and
> estates.* [8]

The government was anything but
supportive of this privately run military.
But the militia operated into the summer of 1748 until
the threats had diminished and the colonies seemed
secure.

As the militia dissolved, Franklin was ready to enter
a new phase in his life. He had made enough money as
a printer and publisher to be financially secure. He felt
so secure that he decided to retire from business
altogether.

At age 42, Franklin's aim was to spend his remaining
years dedicating considerable time to studying science,
literature, and whatever else inspired him along the
way. Little did he know that he still had half his life
ahead of him.

The militia was called up in 1754 for the French and Indian War.

Benjamin Franklin in his forties

FRANKLIN THE SCIENTIST

Even though Franklin retired in 1748 at the age of 42, he had no plans to slow down. He had succeeded in business by working harder, and smarter, than everyone else, while staying true to his ideals. He would succeed in "retirement" in much the same way. He had come to the precise midpoint of his long, productive life, and he still had much to do.

THE SCIENTIST

The next 20 years provided Franklin with many opportunities. Some of his favorite endeavors centered on the scientific explorations he had long wanted to undertake.

Passionate about scientific discovery, Franklin had always exhibited a flair for inventing just the right tool for the job. He loved experimenting and finding a solution to any problem.

As a child who wanted to move faster in the water, he had created swim fins and an early windsurfing apparatus. As a tradesman who wanted to produce publications faster and better, he had created innovations to the printing process. And as a homeowner wanting to stop the black smoke that rolled into the sitting area from his fireplace, he had created a new energy-efficient stove that sent the smoke where it belonged— through the chimney.

An Apple a Day
Franklin did not invent or discover vitamin C, but he was among the first to recognize that foods commonly containing it helped maintain good health. He particularly encouraged the public to eat citrus fruits and apples.

Franklin's model of his Pennsylvania Fireplace, now called the Franklin stove

That stove was called the Pennsylvania Fireplace (and later called the Franklin stove). Although it turned into an important, useful product, Franklin never filed for a patent and thus made little money on it. As far as he was concerned, he was happy to have solved his own heating problem and thrilled to share that solution with others.

Other inventions and innovations credited to Franklin include the glass armonica, library chair, bifocals, catheter, odometer, and the three-wheel clock. Each invention grew out of a specific need. When Franklin saw a need, he did not complain that something did not exist—he simply worked to create what he needed.

LIGHTNING STRIKES

In his first few post-retirement years, Franklin was deeply involved in the work that would lead to his most famous scientific experiments with electricity. Without a business to run, he had the time to fully indulge himself in experimentation. His 1749 journal lists the following 13 observations that made him believe lightning was a naturally occurring form of electricity.

1. *Giving light*
2. *Colour of the light*
3. *Crooked directions*
4. *Swift motion*
5. *Being conducted by metals*
6. *Crack or noise in exploding*

The First Political Cartoon

Franklin has also been credited for inventing the art of the political cartoon for the May 9, 1754, issue of the *Pennsylvania Gazette*. He wrote an editorial regarding the lack of unity among the colonies and added the cartoon for emphasis. He hoped to promote the idea of one national government made up of individual states that had the power to enforce their own policies.

The artwork in the cartoon was a woodcut drawing titled *Join, or Die*. It shows a snake divided in pieces labeled with the colonies' initials. The drawing was based on a popular bit of folk wisdom that said a snake that had been cut in two would come back to life if you reconnected its pieces before sunset. The eight pieces in Franklin's cartoon represented the various colonial governments. The message was that this was the time to unite the colonies.

7. *Subsisting in water or ice*

8. *Rending bodies as it passes through*

9. *Destroying animals*

10. *Melting metals*

11. *Firing inflammable substances*

12. *Sulpherous smell*

13. *The electrical fluid is attracted by points*[2]

In a series of letters to his friend, London merchant and naturalist Peter Collinson, Franklin discussed his belief that electrical charges were both positive and negative in nature. He also presented his theory about lightning as a form of electricity. These letters formed the basis for Franklin's 1751 book *Experiments and Observations on Electricity*. It was popular with readers from all over the world and is considered one of the most important scientific books of the 1700s.

One of his inventions during this exciting time was the lightning rod, which protected people's homes and other buildings from the threat of fire.

In the spring of 1752, a French scientist conducted a lightning rod experiment that Franklin had outlined in his writings. Franklin's theory was proven correct.

During a storm, lightning had struck the rod and safely channeled the electricity into the ground. With the feeling of security that the lightning rod provided, people felt safer during electrical storms. The rods were added to homes, churches, and barns. Interestingly, the lightning rods used today are relatively unchanged from the model Franklin introduced more than 250 years ago.

LIGHTNING STRIKES TWICE?

The story most closely associated with Franklin's investigations into electricity is the legendary kite experiment. Whether it really occurred is a matter of debate. There is no way to prove or disprove it. But Franklin's account of the experiment was published in an October 1752 letter. By this time, news of the French lightning rod experiment had spread. Franklin reported that he had conducted his own experiment in June prior to learning of the French experiment.

Franklin had originally wanted to test his lightning-rod theory using the new steeple of Philadelphia's Christ Church. But construction was slow, and

Franklin grew impatient. So he seized the opportunity of stormy weather and attached metal that attracted electricity to a silk kite. Legend has it that he put a wire at the top of the kite and a key at the base of the wet string. His 21-year-old son William flew the kite while Franklin watched. Reportedly, the string reacted to a lightning strike, and Franklin drew sparks by placing his knuckle on the key. Luckily for the Franklin men, the electrical charge was weak enough that they were not harmed.

Philadelphians reacted to the news of Franklin's amazing test by flocking to his

An Inventive Mind

Franklin's natural curiosity and drive led him to invent and improve upon many common items. Some, such as the lightning rod and Franklin stove, are well known. Other inventions include:

Glass armonica: Also called a glass harmonica, this musical instrument was immediately embraced by the music world. Franklin came up with the idea after attending a concert in which a performer made beautiful music by "playing" a series of glasses of varying shapes and sizes. Franklin loved the sound so much that he set to work building a more practical instrument.

Library chair: Franklin spent lots of time reading, and he wanted to be comfortable. He modified his library chair to include a foot-pedal-operated fan and an adjustable seat. The seat innovation allowed its user to turn it into a secure stepping stool.

Catheter: This is a thin tube which is inserted into the body to allow fluids to pass through it. Franklin improved upon a European version to create the first catheter in America for his ailing brother.

Odometer: In his efforts to improve the postal service, Franklin invented the odometer. This device could measure the distance traveled between two points.

home. They hoped to catch a glimpse of his greatness. The colleges of Harvard, Yale, and William & Mary awarded him—a man with no formal education—special honorary degrees to mark the significance of his discoveries. He was the closest thing to a celebrity one could find in that era.

The Kite Experiment
Most illustrations of Franklin's famous kite experiment show him conducting the test (and the electricity) by himself. But according to his personal account of the experience, his son William flew the kite.

Did the kite experiment take place? Does it really matter? Either way, the image of Benjamin Franklin flying a kite remains a powerful symbol of his very real contributions to the science of electricity.

More Than a Scientist

The rest of the 1750s and the 1760s were busy for Franklin, as always. His interest in science continued, as did his tradition of public service and passion for writing. In 1751, Franklin and Dr. Thomas Bond established the Pennsylvania Hospital—the first hospital in colonial America. Among other things, Franklin was appointed Deputy Postmaster General of North America. He organized troops during the French and Indian War, he wrote his final edition of *Poor Richard's Almanack*, and he traveled to London to work on a

Bifocals

Franklin tired of wearing one pair of glasses for reading and another pair for distance vision. Always inventive, he came up with a solution. He cut the lenses of each pair of glasses in half and combined the halves to create new lenses for a single set of frames. This allowed him to wear just one pair of glasses. Franklin would look through the bottom half of the glasses to focus on his reading and look through the top half to see things further away.

possible change in colonial government.

It may have been hard to envision then, but in the coming decades, Franklin's fame as a printer, colonial leader, and a scientist would rank behind some of his greatest achievements as a noted diplomat, statesman, and Founding Father of the future United States of America. ⌐

Franklin flying a kite to test his theory of the electrical nature of lightning

Benjamin Franklin

A Diplomat, a Patriot, and a Spy

In 1771 at the age of 65, Franklin began writing a letter to his son William. The two had not seen each other for seven years, and Franklin longed to reach out to him. Their opposing political views had caused a rift in their relationship.

Franklin was a staunch supporter of colonial rights and independence from Britain. He was part of the Patriot group during the Revolutionary War era. William, the last colonial governor of New Jersey, was a Loyalist to the end. He wished to remain a devoted subject of the British crown.

THE AUTOBIOGRAPHY

Franklin was getting older, and he missed his son. The two had once been very close. But distance and their political differences had changed all that. He thought he might write William a letter to pass along his life lessons and experiences in case they never spoke again. But the letter project quickly blossomed into a full-length memoir.

Few true autobiographies existed at the time, so Franklin likely gave little or no thought to what such a work should contain. He simply wanted to reflect upon and record his favorite stories for future generations. A talented writer, he enjoyed sharing his experiences from business, public service, and life in general. Most people who write their life story do so

"Remember not only to say the right thing in the right place, but far more difficult still, to leave unsaid the wrong thing at the tempting moment."[1]

—*Benjamin Franklin*

just once, and usually at a time when they think they have made their most significant accomplishments or discoveries. Perhaps Franklin had felt he had passed his peak when he started writing. But his life continued to unfold in exciting ways. His work for the colonies soon took up so much time that he put the autobiography on hold until 1784. He finished writing it in August 1788, about two years before his death.

Stamp Act and Boston Tea Party

Between 1757 and 1775, Franklin spent most of his time in London. He was there as a diplomat trying to save the colonies' relationship with Great Britain. The colonists were considered British citizens, and as such, subjects of the crown. England charged steep, unfair taxes and imposed other policies that interfered with colonists' rights. What started out as a temporary mission for Franklin stretched out over 17 years.

While in London, Franklin promoted the colonists' point of view through articles in English publications. In 1765, England established the Stamp Act, which taxed the colonies on all types of papers, such as almanacs, cards, and newspapers. Angry colonists protested with riots. Franklin tried to smooth things over with the British government. The Stamp Act was

Stamp Act protestors burning stamps in New York City before the American Revolution

finally repealed in March 1766 after colonists boycotted British products.

When England imposed a high tax on tea several years later, the colonists revolted again. They were fed up with

England taking advantage of them. They protested by organizing what has become known as the Boston Tea Party, one of the most important events in early American history. On the night of December 16, 1773, three units of 50 men each dressed up as Mohawk Indians. They boarded three British ships in the Boston Harbor and emptied enormous chests of tea into the water. News of the rebellion quickly spread to other ports, leading other colonist groups to take similar actions.

For a long time, Franklin held out

Declaring Independence

The following excerpt is from the official version of the Declaration of Independence:

IN CONGRESS, July 4, 1776.

When in the Course of human events, it becomes necessary for one people to dissolve the political bands which have connected them with another, and to assume among the powers of the earth, the separate and equal station to which the Laws of Nature and of Nature's God entitle them, a decent respect to the opinions of mankind requires that they should declare the causes which impel them to the separation.--We hold these truths to be self-evident, that all men are created equal, that they are endowed by their Creator with certain unalienable Rights, that among these are Life, Liberty and the pursuit of Happiness.--That to secure these rights, Governments are instituted among Men, deriving their just powers from the consent of the governed,--That whenever any Form of Government becomes destructive of these ends, it is the Right of the People to alter or to abolish it, and to institute new Government, laying its foundation on such principles and organizing its powers in such form, as to them shall seem most likely to effect their Safety and Happiness.[2]

hope that the colonies could remain part of the British Empire while acting as self-governing nations. After all, England was the "mother country," and colonists still felt strong ties. But Britain wanted no part of allowing the colonies to govern themselves. They were ready to fight to keep control—and the colonists were ready to fight back. The seeds of the American Revolution had been planted. There would be no turning back.

CONTINENTAL CONGRESS

Franklin returned to Philadelphia in 1775, but it was too late to see his wife Deborah one last time. After 44 years of marriage, she died on December 19, 1774. Because Deborah feared sea travel, she had never accompanied Ben on any of his many trips abroad. Although they regularly exchanged letters, they rarely saw each other during Deborah's final years. Franklin led a full and exciting life in the heart of London's political and social scenes. Deborah carried on her life as a Philadelphia housewife in the home they had shared.

Franklin was selected by the Pennsylvania government to serve as a

A Spy
During the Revolutionary War era, Franklin served the colonies as a Patriot spy to secretly track its enemies. The purpose of espionage is to gather information that the government can use to protect its citizens, national security, and the economy.

delegate to the Continental Congress. He
was one of the members of its Committee of
Secret Correspondence in late 1775. His
duties included espionage. Along with
George Washington, Franklin served as a
Patriot spy.

Franklin was well respected in Europe,
so the Continental Congress sent him on
a fact-finding mission to Paris, France.
His celebrity gave him access to many people
and made it easier for him to gather the
information he needed. Some methods
Franklin used to collect information are
similar to those used today. For example,
he worked with codes, invisible ink, and
a variety of items to store and pass along
important secret messages.

Espionage
The Committee of Secret
Correspondence was a
forerunner of the modern
CIA, or Central Intelli-
gence Agency.

As an important member
of the Continental Congress,
Franklin also worked on the
Declaration of Independence.
Franklin, along with Thomas Jefferson,
John Adams, Roger Sherman, and
Robert Livingston, had been appointed
by the Continental Congress as the

The Declaration of Independence was approved by the Continental Congress on July 4, 1776.

Committee of Five. They were responsible for writing the statement that would present the colonies' case for being granted independence from England. Jefferson accepted the task of writing the declaration based on the

Franklin's Autobiography

Franklin started writing his autobiography in 1771. But his busy life interfered with his writing, and he abandoned the book until the 1780s. The first edition was published in Paris in 1791, one year after Franklin's death. *The Private Life of the Late Benjamin Franklin, LL*, was translated into English and published in London in 1793.

arguments presented by the Committee of Five. This document, the most essential to the formation of the United States, was drafted by Thomas Jefferson between June 11 and June 28, 1776. It summarized the philosophy behind the colonies' desire to break ties with Great Britain and the rule of King George III. Jefferson gave an early copy to Franklin, who then provided many suggestions that were added to the final version that led to the founding of the United States of America.

The Declaration of Independence

Franklin negotiates a French alliance with Louis XVI.

A Homecoming and
a Farewell

Benjamin Franklin led a remarkable life, and in his last 15 years he engaged in some of his most important work. He was admired at home and abroad as an American statesman and Founding Father. During this period, he distinguished himself as the only person to sign four of the founding documents of the United States. And, in typical Franklin fashion, he lived out his final years with a lust for a life filled with satisfying work, grand distractions, and gentle humor.

PHILADELPHIA HOMECOMING

Having spent several years as a diplomat in Paris during the American Revolution, Franklin was ready to come home. Jefferson was appointed to replace him. Franklin set sail for Philadelphia in May 1785 on what would be his final ocean voyage. All of Philadelphia, including his daughter Sally, turned out to cheer the Revolutionary hero and welcome back their most treasured citizen. He was greeted with a cannon salute and ringing bells—Philadelphia's hero was home at last.

About his homecoming, Franklin wrote, "we were received by a crowd of

Founding Fathers

Franklin was fully involved in all aspects of the founding of the United States. And, he was the only person to sign all four of these historic documents:

• The Declaration of Independence (1776) declared the American colonies independence from English rule.
• The Treaty of Alliance with France (1778) documented France's agreement to help the colonies fight England with troops, arms, and money.
• The Treaty of Paris (1783) marked the official recognition of U.S. independence, ending the American Revolution.
• The Constitution of the United States of America (1787) defined the U.S. government and the basic rights of its citizens.

people with huzzas and accompanied with acclamations quite to my door."[1] And, "The affectionate welcome I meet with from my fellow citizens is far beyond my expectation."[2]

Franklin was now 79 years old, an old man by eighteenth-century standards. He suffered from gout, kidney stones, and other ailments. He had retired from business nearly 40 years prior, yet there still was work to be done.

Of course, there was time to socialize, too. Franklin's many friends, including James Madison and George Washington, were frequent guests at his beautiful home on Market Street. Sally and her family lived with Franklin, and there was always lots of activity. When he was not entertaining visitors, enjoying his gardens, or playing with his grandchildren, Franklin spent his time reading or writing.

Still a voracious reader into his eighties, Franklin never had to go far to choose a new topic. He had built his own massive library with a vast collection of more than 4,000 books.

Saving Time

Franklin proposed the concept of Daylight Saving Time while in Paris in 1784. This is the practice of moving clocks ahead by one hour in the spring (and back again in the fall).

Franklin realized that by doing this, people could take better advantage of the daylight hours during the summer months. He also determined it would mean less use of lamp oil and candles, which would also save money.

U.S. CONSTITUTION

During the sweltering summer of 1787, Franklin and his fellow delegates to the Constitutional Convention met to draft the document that would describe the new nation's government and specify citizens' rights. That document became the Constitution of the United States of America.

Franklin was so ill that he needed help getting to and from the meeting hall. He was twice the average age of the other delegates. But that did not stop him from putting his stamp on the process. He also opened his home as a place for the delegates to take a break from their difficult task.

Franklin was well regarded by all members of the Convention. His experiences as a diplomat, postmaster, and businessman had given him an impressive understanding of both the European and colonial perspectives. The delegates enjoyed listening to the many stories he told to support his opinions. And with Franklin's help, the final document was signed in

We the People

Franklin was one of the signers of the U.S. Constitution. Its introduction, or preamble, describes the document's purpose within the context of the newly formed nation:

"We the People of the United States, in Order to form a more perfect Union, establish Justice, insure domestic Tranquility, provide for the common defence, promote the general Welfare, and secure the Blessings of Liberty to ourselves and our Posterity, do ordain and establish this Constitution for the United States of America."[3]

September 1787 and fully enacted in 1789. He was
feeling his age, but he was thrilled and proud to take
part in establishing the government of the nation for
which he had fought.

Ben A to Z

Franklin's accomplishments are astounding.
While it is difficult to summarize Franklin's life and
contributions, the following is a partial A to Z list
compiled by PBS.org to describe this great man.

A	Abolitionist; Almanac maker
B	Balloon enthusiast; Bifocals inventor
C	Composer; Cartoonist
D	Diplomat; Daylight Savings advocate
E	Electricity pioneer; Experimenter
F	Founding Father; Fire fighter
G	Glass armonica creator
H	Humorist
I	Inventor
J	Junto creator; Journalist
K	Kite flyer
L	Librarian; Lightning rod inventor
M	Medical engineer; Militia member
N	Natural philosopher
O	Organizer; Odometer maker
P	Printer; Publisher
Q	Quartermaster
R	Revolutionary; Reader
S	Scientist; Swimmer
T	Traveler; Treaty signer
U	University builder
V	Volunteer; Visionary
W	Writer
X	Xenophile
Y	Yankee; Yarn spinner
Z	Zealot[4]

THE END OF AN ERA

Franklin was 84 and had been in ill health for some time. Jefferson was one of his last visitors, and Franklin gave him a copy of his unpublished autobiography as a memento. With his grandchildren at his side, Benjamin Franklin died on April 17, 1790.

Franklin was buried next to his wife Deborah at

Philadelphia's Christ Church cemetery. In typical Franklin fashion, as a 22-year-old printer intent on carving out a virtuous life, Franklin had written his own epitaph years earlier:

Ahead of His Time
In one of Franklin's last political acts, the one-time slave owner wrote an article for the abolition of slavery. His stance was ahead of its time. It would be another 75 years before the Emancipation Proclamation freed the slaves.

The Body of
B. Franklin, Printer;
(Like the cover of an old book,
Its contents torn out,
And stript of its lettering and gilding)
Lies here, food for worms.
But the work shall not be lost;
For it will (as he believed), appear
once more,
In a new and more elegant edition,
Revised and corrected
By the Author [5]

Those words might well have seemed suitable had he come across them again some 60-odd years later as he revised his will. But instead, he asked to have this simple message inscribed on his tombstone:

Benjamin and Deborah Franklin: 1790. [6]

More than 20,000 people gathered to mourn Franklin's death on the day of his funeral. The citizens of Philadelphia cried out and comforted each other as they watched his funeral procession make its way to the burial grounds.

It was difficult to say good-bye to this great man. He had meant so much to so many for the better part of a century. And the impact of Franklin's life was only just beginning to be realized. That his passing brought forth such a monumental response was a testament to his legacy as a revered Philadelphian, a prized American, and an esteemed citizen of the world. It is a legacy that continues to this day.

"Dr. Franklin is well known to be the greatest philosopher of the present age; all the operations of nature he seems to understand, the very heavens obey him, and the clouds yield up their lightning to be imprisoned in his rod. ... a most extraordinary man, and tells a story in a style more engaging than anything I have ever heard."[7]

—William Pierce

Gravestones at the historic Christ Church Burial Ground where Benjamin Franklin is buried.

TIMELINE

1706	1718	1722	1723
Benjamin Franklin is born in Boston January 17.	Franklin is apprenticed to his brother's printing shop.	Franklin's first Silence Dogood letter is published April 2.	Franklin runs away to New York September 25.

1728	1729	1730	1731
Franklin opens a printing shop in Philadelphia.	Franklin buys the *Pennsylvania Gazette*.	Franklin enters a common-law marriage with Deborah Read September 1.	Franklin founds the Library Company of Philadelphia July 1.

1723

Franklin arrives in Philadelphia October 8.

1724

Franklin moves to London.

1726

Franklin returns to Philadelphia in July.

1727

Franklin forms the Junto club.

1732

Franklin's son Francis "Franky" is born. Franklin publishes the first *Poor Richard's Almanack*.

1736

Franklin's son Francis dies of smallpox. Franklin forms the Union Fire Company.

1737

Franklin is appointed Philadelphia postmaster.

1743

Franklin's daughter Sarah "Sally" is born. Franklin founds the American Philosophical Society.

TIMELINE

1747	1748	1749	1751
Franklin writes *Plain Truth*. Franklin organizes the Pennsylvania Militia.	Franklin retires from active business.	Franklin proposes the academy that becomes the University of Pennsylvania.	Franklin's *Experiments and Observations on Electricity* is published in April.

1771	1774	1775	1776
Franklin begins writing his autobiography.	Deborah Franklin dies December 19.	Franklin is elected to the Second Continental Congress May 6.	Franklin signs the Declaration of Independence.

1751

Franklin and Dr. Thomas Bond establish the first hospital in colonial America May 11.

1752

Franklin performs his legendary kite experiment.

1753

Franklin is appointed joint Deputy Postmaster for America August 10.

1757

Franklin writes the final *Poor Richard's Almanack*.

1778

Franklin negotiates the Treaty of Alliance with France.

1783

Franklin signs the Treaty of Paris that marks the official recognition of U.S. independence, ending the American Revolution.

1787

Franklin signs the U.S. Constitution.

1790

Benjamin Franklin dies in Philadelphia April 17.

Essential Facts

Date of Birth
January 17, 1706

Place of Birth
Boston, Massachusetts

Date of Death
April 17, 1790

Place of Death
Philadelphia, Pennsylvania

Parents
Josiah and Abiah Franklin

Education
Boston Latin School and a writing and reading academy; no formal education after the age of ten

Marriage
Common-law marriage to Deborah Read in 1730

Children
William Franklin, Francis Franklin, and Sarah Franklin

Career Highlights
Owned the *Pennsylvania Gazette*; published *Poor Richard's Almanack*; organized the Pennsylvania militia; served as a diplomat to Great Britain; and was a delegate to the Constitutional Convention that drafted the U.S. Constitution

Societal Contribution
With Dr. Bond, Franklin established the Pennsylvania Hospital— the first hospital in colonial America; founded the Library Company of Philadelphia; proposed the academy of learning that became the University of Pennsylvania

Residences
Boston, Philadelphia, and London

Travels
London and France as a diplomat

Conflicts
Early conflicts as an apprentice to his brother James; as a Patriot, Franklin had conflicts with his son William, a staunch Loyalist.

Quote
"Remember not only to say the right thing in the right place, but far more difficult still, to leave unsaid the wrong thing at the tempting moment."—*Benjamin Franklin*

ADDITIONAL RESOURCES

SELECT BIBLIOGRAPHY

Chaplin, Joyce E. *The First Scientific American: Benjamin Franklin and the Pursuit of Genius.* New York: Basic Books, 2006.

Isaacson, Walter. *Benjamin Franklin: An American Life.* New York: Simon & Schuster, 2003.

Isaacson, Walter. *A Benjamin Franklin Reader.* New York: Simon & Schuster, 2003.

Rogers, George L., ed. *Benjamin Franklin's The Art of Virtue.* Midvale, UT: Choice Skills, 1996.

Tucker, Tom. *Bolt of Lightning: Benjamin Franklin and His Fabulous Kite.* New York: Public Affairs, 2003.

Wood, Gordon S. *The Americanization of Benjamin Franklin.* New York: The Penguin Press, 2004.

FURTHER READING

Collier, James Lincoln. *The Benjamin Franklin You Never Knew.* New York: Children's Press, 2004.

TIME for Kids, eds., with Kathryn Hoffman Satterfield. *Benjamin Franklin: A Man of Many Talents.* New York: HarperCollins, 2005.

Whiting, Jim. *The Life and Times of Benjamin Franklin.* Hockessin, DE: Mitchell Lane, 2006.

Web Links

To learn more about Benjamin Franklin, visit ABDO Publishing Company on the World Wide Web at **www.abdopublishing.com**. Web sites about Benjamin Franklin are featured on our Book Links page. These links are routinely monitored and updated to provide the most current information available.

Places to Visit

The Benjamin Franklin House
36 Craven Street, London, UK W2CN 5NF
44 (0)20 7930 6601
www.benjaminfranklinhouse.org
Franklin lived here during his time in London as a diplomat.
This is the only home that Franklin lived in that still exists.
Performances and hands-on displays offer a glimpse into Franklin's life.

Franklin Court
Historic District, Philadelphia, PA
215-597-1785
www.nps.gov/inde/franklin-court.htm
Visit the Franklin Museum relating to Franklin's print shop, inventions, Post Office, and demonstrations of eighteenth-century printing techniques.

Independence Hall in Philadelphia
Chestnut Street between 5th and 6th Streets
Philadelphia, PA 19102
215-965-2305
www.gophila.com/C/Things_to_Do/211/Philadelphia_CultureFiles/
Initially built as the Pennsylvania State House, it later took on the name Independence Hall. This is where the Declaration of Independence was adopted and the U.S. Constitution discussed, written, and signed.

GLOSSARY

abroad
Living or working outside of one's country.

apprentice
One who works with a skilled professional to learn a trade.

artisan
One who hand-crafts items.

boycott
Express disapproval by refusing to buy a product or deal with someone.

controversial
An issue marked with opposing viewpoints.

currency
Coin or paper money.

denomination
The value or worth of currency.

diplomat
One who practices the art of compromise.

dissertation
Written treatment of a subject.

epitaph
A brief statement in memory of a person.

espionage
The practice of spying.

gazette
A newspaper.

innovation
A new idea, method, or device.

inoculate
Protect from disease by injecting a small amount of the organism so the body builds immunity to it.

memoir
A narrative of one's personal experiences.

militia
A group of citizens organized for military service.

navigation
Method of determining position, course, and distance traveled.

patriot
One who loves his country and supports its interests.

polygamist
One who has more than one spouse at a given time.

pseudonym
False or fictitious name.

statesman
A person who conducts the business of a government.

typesetting
To compose type for printing.

vaccine
A preparation administered to increase immunity to a disease.

xenophile
Attracted to foreign ideas, styles, or things.

zealot
Person with a cause or ideal.

SOURCE NOTES

Chapter 1. A Self-made Man

1. J.A. Leo Lemay, ed. *Franklin Writings*. New York: Library Classics, 1987. 1313.

Chapter 2. Learning a Trade

None.

Chapter 3. On His Own

1. Walter Isaacson. *A Benjamin Franklin Reader*. New York: Simon & Schuster, 2003. 35.
2. Walter Isaacson. *Benjamin Franklin: An American Life*. New York: Simon & Schuster, 2003. 37.
3. Walter Isaacson. *A Benjamin Franklin Reader*. New York: Simon & Schuster, 2003. 33.

Chapter 4. Back in Philadelphia

1. J.A. Leo Lemay, ed. *Franklin Writings*. New York: Library Classics, 1987.
2. Carl Van Doren. *Benjamin Franklin*. New York: Simon Publications, 2002. 90-91.
3. J.A. Leo Lemay, ed. *Franklin Writings*. New York: Library Classics, 1987.
4. Benjamin Franklin. *Poor Richard's Almanack*. Mount Vernon, NY: Peter Pauper Press, 1992. 45.

Chapter 5. Reading and Writing

1. David B. Gracy II, ed. "Library Company of Philadelphia." *Libraries & the Cultural Record.* School of Information, 8 May 2007. School of Information, The University of Texas at Austin. 21 May 2007 <http://www.gslis.utexas.edu/~landc/bookplates/12_2_LibCoPhilly.htm>.
2. J.A. Leo Lemay, ed. *Franklin Writings*. New York: Library Classics, 1987. 1380.

3. Walter Isaacson. *Benjamin Franklin: An American Life*. New York: Simon &
Schuster, 2003. 95.
4. Ben Franklin. "The Quotable Franklin." *The Electric Ben Franklin*.
Independence Hall Association. 21 May 2007. http://www.ushistory.org/
franklin/quotable/singlehtml.htm.
5. *Pages of 1733 Poor Richard's Almanack*. 31 Jan. 2001. 21 May 2007
<http://www3.gettysburg.edu/~tshannon/his341/pra1733pg5.htm>.
6. *Benjamin Franklin Writer and Printer*. The Library Company of Philadelphia. 21
May 2007 <http://www.librarycompany.org/BFWriter/wealth.htm>.
7. J.A. Leo Lemay, ed. *Franklin Writings*. New York: Library Classics, 1987. 1397.

Chapter 6. Community Service

1. Benjamin Franklin. "The Quotable Franklin." *The Electric Ben Franklin*.
Independence Hall Association. 21 May 2007 <http://www.ushistory.org/
franklin/quotable/singlehtml.htm>.
2. Walter Isaacson. *Benjamin Franklin: An American Life*. New York: Simon &
Schuster, 2003. 83.
3. "U.S. Postal Service Commemorates Benjamin Franklin's 300th Birthday
by Issuing Educational Stamps This Spring." United States Postal Service. 17
Jan. 2006 <http://www.usps.com/communications/news/stamps/2006
/sr06_004.htm>.
4. Walter Isaacson. *Benjamin Franklin: An American Life*. New York: Simon &
Schuster, 2003. 115.
5. Benjamin Franklin. "A Letter to Abiah Franklin." *The Papers of Benjamin
Franklin*. 21 May 2007 <http://franklinpapers.org/franklin/
framedVolumes.jsp?vol=3&page=474a>.
6. Walter Isaacson. *A Benjamin Franklin Reader*. New York: Simon & Schuster,
2003. 134.
7. Ibid. 124.
8. Ibid. 126.

Chapter 7. Franklin the Scientist

1. "Essays, Articles and Miscellany: Franklin's Favorite Foods." *Benjamin Franklin Tercentenary*. 21 May 2007 <http://www.benfranklin300.com/etc_article_foods.htm>.
2. "Franklin the Scientist." Department of Mathematics, Texas A & M University. 21 May 2007 <http://www. math.tamu.edu/~stecher/489/Ben/science.shtml>.

Chapter 8. A Diplomat, a Patriot, and a Spy

1. Benjamin Franklin. *ThinkExist.com Quotations*. 21 May 2007 <http://thinkexist.com/quotes/with/keyword/right_thing>.
2. "Declaration of Independence." *National Archives Experience, Charters of Freedom*. 21 May 2007 <http://www.archives.gov/national-archives-experience/charters/constitution_transcript.html>.

Chapter 9. A Homecoming and a Farewell

1. Walter Isaacson. *Benjamin Franklin: An American Life*. New York: Simon & Schuster, 2003. 437.
2. Ibid. 438.
3. "Declaration of Independence." *The Founders' Constitution*. Volume 2, Preamble, Document 4. The University of Chicago Press. 21 May 2007 <http://press-pubs.uchicago.edu/founders/documents/preambles4.html>.
4. "Ben A to Z." *Benjamin Franklin*. Public Broadcasting Service (PBS). 21 May 2007 <http://www.pbs.org/benfranklin/az.html>.
5. Walter Isaacson. *Benjamin Franklin: An American Life*. New York: Simon & Schuster, 2003. 470.
6. "Christ Church Burial Ground." Historic Christ Church and Burial Ground, Philadelphia Web site. 2006. 6 June 2007. <http://www.oldchristchurch.org/burial/>.
7. Walter Isaacson. *Benjamin Franklin: An American Life*. New York: Simon & Schuster, 2003. 446.

Index

Index Continued

ABOUT THE AUTHOR

L.L. Owens grew up in the Midwest and studied English and Journalism in college before launching a career in publishing. She has authored more than 50 books for young readers and particularly loves to write informational books, historical fiction, and retellings of classic literature. Recent titles include the biography *Abraham Lincoln: A Great American Life*; the Civil War story *Brothers at War*; and a graphic novel retelling of Victor Hugo's *The Hunchback of Notre Dame*.

PHOTO CREDITS